BOSTON COMMON PRESS
Brookline, Massachusetts

2000

Other titles in the *Cook's Illustrated*
How to Cook Series

HOW TO MAKE MUFFINS, BISCUITS, & SCONES

An illustrated step-by-step guide to
foolproof cornbread, Irish soda bread,
banana bread, and other
simple baked goods.

THE COOK'S ILLUSTRATED LIBRARY

Illustrations by John Burgoyne

Boston Common Press
17 Station Street
Brookline, Massachusetts 02445

ISBN 0-936184-46-9
Library of Congress Cataloging-in-Publication Data
The Editors of *Cook's Illustrated*
How to make muffins, biscuits, and scones: An illustrated step-by-step guide to foolproof cornbread, Irish soda bread, banana bread, and other simple baked goods./
The Editors of *Cook's Illustrated*
1st ed.

Includes 32 recipes and 12 illustrations
ISBN 0-936184-46-9 (hardback): $14.95
I. Cooking. I. Title
2000

Manufactured in the United States of America

Distributed by Boston Common Press, 17 Station Street, Brookline, MA 02445.

Cover and text design: Amy Klee
Recipe development: Elizabeth Germain
Series editor: Jack Bishop

CONTENTS

introduction

QUICK BREADS HAVE PLENTY OF APPEAL FOR the modern cook. They can be made in a matter of minutes, yet the pay-off is high. Who doesn't love a good blueberry muffin or a basket of warm biscuits served with dinner?

Although quick breads—a category of baked goods leavened with baking powder and/or soda rather than yeast—are easy to prepare, many things can still go wrong. Who hasn't made biscuits that were tough or muffins that were dry and bland?

For this book, we went into our test kitchen to perfect recipes for muffins, biscuits, and scones as well as other quick breads, including Irish soda bread, banana bread, cornbread, and cranberry-nut bread. Many of our findings were surprising.

Muffin recipes often instruct the cook to assemble the batter the same way you would to make pancakes: Dry and wet ingredients (including melted butter) are whisked in separate bowls, then the dry ingredients are folded into the wet ingredients just until combined. Our tests proved that the most tender, best tasting muffins result when you follow the standard procedure for making a cake. Cream the butter and sugar, beat in the eggs, then add the dry ingredients to the batter alternately with the liquid.

For classic biscuits, cold butter must be rubbed into the flour until the mixture forms small bits of dough. We found that a food processor is a better tool than your hands for this job because the latter can overheat the butter and cause it to melt. However, for cooks who find this step difficult, we developed a biscuit recipe without any butter at all. Cream adds the fat and flavor in this foolproof recipe.

We discovered that the best scones are made like biscuits, but with more sugar for flavor and cream as well as butter for richness. We also found that using really ripe bananas is the key to moist banana bread.

How to Make Muffins, Biscuits, and Scones is the 24th book in the How to Cook series published by *Cook's Illustrated*, a bimonthly publication on American home cooking. Turn to the beginning of the book for a complete list of the titles in the series. To order other books, call us at (800) 611-0759 or visit us online at www.cooksillustrated.com. For a free trial copy of *Cook's*, call (800) 526-8442.

Christopher P. Kimball
Publisher and Editor
Cook's Illustrated

chapter one

QUICK BREAD BASICS

UFFINS, BISCUITS, SCONES, CORNBREAD, banana bread, and Irish soda bread have a number of elements in common. All of these baked goods can be quickly prepared (the batter or dough can usually be assembled in the time it takes to preheat the oven) and quickly baked. This sets them far apart from yeast breads, which must be allowed to rise for hours before baking. Chemical leaveners, such as baking powder and baking soda, are speedy and reliable.

There are a number of ingredients, pieces of equipment, and techniques you will use repeatedly when making recipes in this book.

INGREDIENTS

∷ BUTTER

For flavor, butter is the best fat to use in muffins, biscuits, and quick breads. We tested leading brands and found that freshness is the factor that most affects flavor. The best way to store butter is sealed in an airtight plastic bag in the freezer, pulling out sticks as you need them. Butter will keep in the freezer for several months but for no more than two or three weeks in the refrigerator.

We use unsalted butter in our test kitchen. We like its sweet, delicate flavor and prefer to add our own salt to recipes. We find that the quality of salted butter is often inferior and that each manufacturer adds a different amount of salt, which makes recipe writing difficult.

∷ DAIRY

Milk, buttermilk, yogurt, or cream is essential to all of the recipes in this book. They help bring doughs together and add flavor and richness.

Buttermilk and yogurt are acidic (both have been treated with bacteria) and will give baked goods a subtle tang. Recipes with these dairy items usually contain baking soda. Use either low-fat or whole-milk plain yogurt, but avoid nonfat yogurt, which can make baked goods a bit dry and bland. Buttermilk is very low in fat—use either regular or skim versions. When measuring thick buttermilk or cream, make sure to use a spatula to scrape all of the liquid out of the measuring cup and into the batter.

⠶ FLOUR

Most of the recipes in this book call for all-purpose flour. All-purpose flour is typically made from a combination of hard red winter wheat and soft red winter wheat. Perhaps the primary difference between these types of wheat—and, consequently, in the flours made from them—is the variation in protein content. Hard winter wheat is about 10 to 13 percent protein, and soft wheat about 8 to 10 percent. Mixtures of the two wheats are somewhere in between.

High-protein flours are generally recommended for yeasted products and other baked goods that require a lot of structural support. The reason is that the higher the protein level in a flour, the greater the potential for the formation of gluten. The sheets that gluten forms in dough are elastic enough to move with the gas released by yeast (which causes the bread to rise) but also sturdy enough to prevent that gas from escaping, so the dough doesn't deflate. Lower-protein flours, on the other hand, are recommended for chemically leavened baked goods such as cakes and pastries. This is because baking powder and baking soda are quick leaveners. They lack the endurance of yeast, which can force the naturally resistant gluten sheets to expand. Gluten can overpower quick leaveners, causing the final baked product to fall flat. For this reason, bread flour (which is made from high-protein wheat) does not work in a muffin or biscuit recipe.

A second important difference in flours is whether they are bleached or not. Technically, all all-purpose flours are bleached. Carotenoid pigments in wheat lend a faint yellowish tint to freshly milled flour. But in a matter of about 12 weeks, these pigments oxidize, undergoing the same chemical process that turns a sliced apple brown. In this case, yellowish flour changes to a whiter hue (though not stark white). Early in this century, as the natural bleaching process came to be understood, scientists identified methods to chemically expedite and intensify it. Typically, all-purpose flours are bleached with either benzoyl peroxide or chlorine gas. The latter not only bleaches the flour but also alters the flour proteins, making them less inclined to form strong gluten. Today many consumers prefer chemically bleached flour over unbleached because they associate the whiter color with higher quality.

In extensive kitchen tests, we found that chemically bleached flour can give simple baked goods an "off" flavor, most often described as metallic. This characteristic is easiest to spot in a simple biscuit and less noticeable in a muffin with lots of sugar and other flavorful ingredients. We prefer unbleached, all-purpose flour for most uses.

In some cases, when we want an especially tender texture, we use cake flour along with the all-purpose. While all-purpose flour is made from hard wheat (at least in part) and contains between 10 and 12 percent protein, cake flour is made from soft wheat and typically has just 8 to 10 percent protein. Less protein means less gluten formation and a more tender crumb.

Most supermarkets sell two kinds of cake flour: plain and self-rising. Self-rising cake flour contains salt and baking powder and is meant to be a convenience product. We would rather choose the amount and type of leavener that goes into our baking.

No matter the type or brand, we measure all flour by the dip-and-sweep method. Dip a metal or plastic dry measure into a bag of flour so that the cup is overflowing with flour. Then use a knife or icing spatula to level off the flour, sweeping the excess back into the bag. Short of weighing flour (which is what professional bakers do), this measuring method is your best guarantee of using the right amount of flour. Spooning the flour into the measuring cup aerates it, and you might end up with as much as 25 percent less flour by weight.

▚ LEAVENERS

Muffins, biscuits, and quick breads, as well as cookies, cakes, pancakes, and waffles, get their rise from chemical leaveners—baking soda and baking powder—rather than yeast. Chemical leavenings react with acids to produce carbon dioxide, the gas that causes these baked goods to rise.

To do its work, baking soda relies on an acidic ingredient in the recipe, such as buttermilk, sour cream, yogurt, or molasses. It's important to use the right amount of baking soda in recipes. Use more baking soda than can be neutralized by the acidic ingredient, and you'll end up with a metallic-tasting, coarse-crumbed quick bread or cake.

Baking powder is nothing more than baking soda (about one-quarter to one-third of the total makeup) mixed with a dry acid and double-dried cornstarch. The cornstarch absorbs moisture and keeps the baking soda and the dry acid apart during storage, preventing premature production of the gas. When baking powder becomes wet, the acid comes into contact with the baking soda, producing carbon dioxide. Most commercial baking powders are "double-acting." In other words, they contain two kinds of acid—one that produces a carbon dioxide reaction at room temperature, the other responding only to heat.

In contrast, baking soda is only single-acting, as is

13

homemade baking powder, which contains only one acid, cream of tartar. Baking soda reacts immediately on contact with an acid. In a muffin, for example, it is important to have an early release of carbon dioxide during the batter preparation so that small bubbles will be created to form the foundation of the cell structure. These cells expand during baking because of additional carbon dioxide production caused by the action of the second leavening acid in baking powder, and the dough firms up into the final muffin structure.

EQUIPMENT

▟ BAKING SHEETS

We tested 11 brands of baking sheets and found that sheets with shiny surfaces do a better job than darker pans, especially those with black nonstick surfaces. We found that scones and biscuits tend to burn on the bottom when baked on dark sheets. We prefer baking sheets that are rimless on at least one side so that baked goods can be slid right onto a cooling rack.

▟ FOOD PROCESSOR

The steel blade on a food processor is the best tool for cutting cold butter into dry ingredients to make biscuits and scones. Choose a large model (an 11-cup workbowl is best) that can handle a full batch of dough. You won't be able to make a dozen biscuits in a small food processor. Also, check out the weight of the base. A 10-pound food processor will stay put on the counter, no matter what kind of dough you are kneading. Lighter models may bounce around when trying to knead stiff yeast bread doughs.

■■ ICE CREAM SCOOP

A spring-loaded ice cream scoop ensures uniform muffin size and clean dispensing when transferring the dough to the holes in a muffin tin. We use an ice cream scoop that holds one-half cup, so one full scoop will fill each hole in a regular muffin tin. If you use an ice cream scoop, don't attempt to smooth out the top of the batter in each muffin hole. The oven heat will do this.

■■ LOAF PANS

In our testing, we found that dark-colored nonstick loaf pans brown banana breads and other quick breads evenly. Breads, especially sweet ones, can burn in glass loaf pans. Also, pans with handles at either end are easier to work with and should prevent you from sticking your oven mitt into the edge of a baked loaf. Even with the nonstick coating, we recommend greasing and flouring your loaf pan to ensure easy release.

▐▐ MIXERS

We find that standing mixers are easy to use (hands are free to add ingredients) and do the best job of beating air into cream, egg whites, and cake batter. For quick breads, though, all that's needed is a handheld mixer.

When shopping for a standing mixer, look for a heavy model with a single paddle-type attachment. Less expensive models that use classic beaters are only a small step up in quality from handheld mixers. Paddle attachments are much better at incorporating ingredients and won't become clogged with batter or dough.

As for handheld mixers, avoid those models with old-fashioned beaters that have a thick post running down the center. Look for beaters with thin, curved wires and open centers. Handles that slope higher in the front and lower in back are easier on your arm.

▐▐ MUFFIN PAPERS

We baked muffins with and without paper liners. Those baked in papers were shorter than those baked right in the cup, but they also had a more rounded, filled-out look. When peeling off the papers, we lost a good portion of the muffin. Muffin papers also keep the muffin's sides from browning as well as those baked right in the cup. We prefer to grease muffin tins instead of using paper liners.

▪▪ MUFFIN TINS

Muffin tins come in a variety of finishes and sizes. As with loaf pans, we found that tins with dark nonstick finishes promote deep browning and are preferred. Each hole in a standard muffin tin can hold about one-half cup of batter.

In our research, we ran across a few recipes with instructions to grease the bottom, but not the sides, of the muffin holes. We tested two batches of muffins—one baked in greased holes, the other baked in holes in which only the bottoms were greased. We observed no difference between those baked in holes that had been greased completely and those baked in holes with greased bottoms only. Since it's difficult to grease the bottom but not the sides of a muffin hole, we just grease the entire hole.

TECHNIQUES

There are several methods commonly used to assemble quick breads. The most common, often referred to as the quick bread method, calls for mixing wet and dry ingredients separately, pouring wet into dry, then mixing them together as quickly as possible. Batters for pancakes, popovers, and many quick breads rely on this approach.

A second technique, often called the creaming method and more common to cake batters, starts with creaming the butter and sugar until light and fluffy. Eggs and flavorings

17

are beaten in, then the dry and liquid ingredients are alternately added. For the best results, we like to cream butter in a tall, narrow bowl.

A third possibility comes from the tradition of biscuit and pie-dough making, in which cold fat is cut into the dry ingredients with fingertips, a fork, a pastry blender, or the blade of a food processor. Once the mixture has achieved a cornmeal-like texture with pea-sized flecks, liquid is added and quickly mixed in.

We have tested these three mixing methods on all of the recipes in this book. Often, we have found that the same ingredients will bake up quite differently depending on how they are combined.

DO-AHEAD TRICK

Muffins, biscuits, scones, and quick breads are morning food. However, many cooks balk at any early-morning baking project. To save time and energy, we found it was possible to measure and mix dry ingredients ahead of time. Simply place the flour, sugar, leavener, and salt in a covered container at room temperature. In the morning, add the butter and dairy items, and the batter will be ready before your oven is preheated.

STORAGE METHODS

When testing recipes for this book, we found ourselves with lots of muffins and biscuits and quick breads on our hands. Invariably, we tried to store them. Here are the results of our tests.

Biscuits and cornbread are the least promising candidates for storage. These baked goods taste best warm, although they are fine at room temperature. However, when stored for more than a few hours, biscuits become soggy and cornbread dries out and crumbles. The refrigerator or freezer is not kind to these items.

Quick breads (Irish soda bread, banana bread, and cranberry-nut bread) are the easiest to store. If wrapped tightly in plastic (once cooled), the breads will stay fresh for a couple of days. Slices are also delicious when toasted, even when not quite fresh.

Muffins and scones are best eaten the day they are made. Once cooled, they can be stored in an airtight container at room temperature. Day-old muffins can be sliced in half and reheated in a toaster oven, with the cut sides facing up. Toast the muffins for four or five minutes, then slather them with butter and/or jam. Scones don't really reheat well and are best eaten at room temperature. Day-old scones will not be as good as fresh ones but are certainly acceptable.

For longer storage, muffins and scones should be frozen in an airtight container. We found that muffins freeze better than scones. That said, a different method should be used for thawing muffins and scones.

We tested thawing both kinds of baked goods on the counter, in a toaster oven, in a warm oven, and in the microwave. Muffins thawed in the toaster oven were doughy and heated unevenly. Muffins thawed in the microwave were damp and, again, heated unevenly. Muffins thawed at room temperature were our least favorite. The outside was soft and mushy, the inside was doughy, and the flavor muted and old tasting.

We found that muffins are best thawed in a 350-degree oven. Place frozen muffins on a baking sheet and then immediately into a preheated oven. Corn muffins take 15 minutes to defrost, classic muffins 20 minutes, and bran 25 minutes. (These are good estimates. To test for doneness, cut a muffin in half from top to bottom and feel the inside. If frozen or still cold, continue heating 3 to 5 minutes more.) Classic and bran muffins make for great eating when treated this way. The crust gets crispier than the exterior of a just-baked muffin and the inside is moist, tender, and full-flavored. The bran muffins are very aromatic. Corn muffins seem to dry out, but they are still acceptable.

Scones thawed in a regular or toaster oven dried out too

much. This was particularly noticeable with oatmeal scones, which became very crumbly. The microwave made the scones soggy. We had the best luck thawing scones on the counter to room temperature. This takes two to three hours and works best with scones that don't have any fresh fruit, which ends up tasting stale after freezing and makes the scones too moist.

chapter two

CLASSIC MUFFINS

AVE YOU EVER TRIED TO BAKE A BATCH OF those jumbo muffins you see in bakeries and specialty coffee shops? If you follow most cookbook recipes, you won't get what you're looking for. We tried scores of recipes, and we weren't satisfied with the results, either. Some muffins came out flat-topped or misshapen. Other batches were either rich and leaden or dense and dry. The best were pleasant, but not outstanding.

Our standards, admittedly, were high. We weren't looking for a "healthy" muffin to incorporate in our daily diet. We wanted a really great weekend muffin, one that would make brunch guests covet the recipe. This muffin had to have it all. It needed rich, full flavor with a thin, crisp crust protecting its fragile, tender crumb. What's more, this muffin had to be a real looker. We would settle for nothing less than a perfectly round, mushroomlike cap with a pronounced, crisp overhang.

Working with a conservative six-muffin recipe, we decided to start our tests with mixing techniques. Our review of recipes pointed to the three possible methods introduced in chapter 1 (quick bread method, creaming method, biscuit/pie dough method; see pages 17–18). Although the recipe we were working with at this point was way too lean (the muffins were small, dry, tough, and unappetizing), it did have one thing going for it—the creaming method. The creamed-batter muffins we had made thus far were more tender-crumbed than their competitors.

We were puzzled at this development. Practically every quick bread recipe cautions not to overmix the batter once wet and dry ingredients have been combined. Better, most authors reason, to leave streaks of flour in the batter than to overdevelop the flour's gluten, which results in smaller, denser, and tougher muffins.

In the creaming method, the batter was beaten by machine up to two minutes, depending on the recipe. If overbeating caused gluten development and tough muffins, why were these muffins tender? The explanation is fairly straightforward. In the creaming process butter is first aerated with sugar, then fat- and moisture-rich eggs are beaten into the mix. Dry ingredients are added alternately with the wet ingredients. In most creamed butter recipes, a good portion of the flour (in our recipe, it's half) is added to the creamed butter mixture before the wet ingredients. That way, the fat from the butter and egg coats most of the flour, preventing any gluten formation. The remaining flour and wet ingredients are added alternately at this point, stimulating only a part of the flour's gluten. Certainly some of the flour's gluten must be activated; otherwise the muffin would have no structure at all.

In the quick-bread method, all wet ingredients and fats are added at once, denying the flour an opportunity to be coated with fat. We naturally questioned why the quick-bread method couldn't approximate the creaming method of coating the flour with fat first. So we made a batch of muffins, mixing the dry ingredients, then adding melted butter and eggs to disperse the fat. When the flour was sufficiently coated, we stirred in the remaining wet ingredient (usually a dairy product, in this case, yogurt).

The muffins were just as tender as those made using the creamed method. But because the batter had not been aerated by the mixer, they lacked the height of the mixer muffins. So when you're short on time, you can achieve more tender muffins by simply mixing the melted butter and eggs into the dry ingredients. The muffins will not rise high enough to develop a lip, but their texture and flavor will be fine. When perfection counts, get out the mixer.

With the mixing method chosen, we moved on to testing individual ingredients. Because our original formula was too dry and savory, we increased the butter and sugar, then moved on to testing the primary ingredient: flour. We made muffins with cake flour, all-purpose flour, and an equal mix of cake and all-purpose flours.

The batter made with cake flour was incredibly loose compared with the other batters, resulting in muffins that were squat, wet, and greasy. They also lacked a distinct, crisp outer crust. Muffins baked with half cake and half all-purpose were a step up from the cake flour muffins, but their texture was a tad wet and greasy and they lacked the beautiful shape of those made entirely with all-purpose flour. Although the all-purpose flour formula still needed work, these muffins were shapely and fairly tender, with a nice contrast between crust and crumb. After our flour tests, we decided that the formula needed more sugar for added flavor.

By now our formula was beginning to take shape, and we were ready to test liquids. We made muffins using low-fat milk, whole milk, half-and-half, cream, powdered milk plus water (common in commercial baking), buttermilk, yogurt, and sour cream. Leavening adjustments were made (reducing the amount of baking powder and including baking soda) for all the buttermilk, yogurt, and sour cream muffins.

The thin liquids—low-fat milk, whole milk, powdered milk, and half-and-half—naturally produced thin batters that baked into smooth-topped muffins. They looked more like cupcakes. Low-fat milk muffins were soufflé-shaped, with straight sides and flat tops.

The thicker liquids—cream, buttermilk, low-fat yogurt, and sour cream—delivered thicker batters and muffins with rounded, textured tops. The higher-fat muffins, particularly those made with sour cream and cream, were squat, dense, heavy, and wet. The buttermilk muffins were good, but the yogurt-enriched were better, having a rough-textured rounded top, a sweet-tangy flavor, and a light, tender crumb.

Now that we had a working base, we started adding fruits and flavorings. Three additional adjustments to the recipe came during this part of the testing. Although the sugar level seemed right in the plain muffin, the muffins made with tart fruit and other ingredients did not seem sweet enough. After increasing the sugar for the fruit variations, we found that we liked more sugar in the plain version of the recipe as well. We also found that one more tablespoon of butter gave us additional tenderness without weighing down the muffin. Increasing the batter by one-half—from a recipe that uses 2 cups of flour to one that uses 3 cups—pumped up the volume to give us not only a beautifully rounded top but also a nice big lip. This base worked with all of the following variations, so you should feel free to plug in your own favorite ingredients.

As a final question, we wondered if the kind of fat used to grease the muffin tin would affect the final baked product. To find out, we baked muffins in an ungreased muffin tin and in four more tins, one each coated in butter, shortening, oil, and vegetable cooking spray. Only those baked in ungreased muffin tins were completely unacceptable, displaying tough, leathery crusts. Although differences were subtle, we preferred the flavor of the muffins baked in buttered tins. For ease and speed, vegetable cooking spray took first place.

Master Recipe

Basic Muffins

makes 1 dozen large muffins

➤ NOTE: *To cinnamon-coat muffin tops, dip warm muffins in melted butter, then in mixture of ½ cup granulated sugar and 2 teaspoons ground cinnamon.*

	Vegetable cooking spray or unsalted butter for greasing muffin tin
3	cups all-purpose flour
1	tablespoon baking powder
½	teaspoon baking soda
½	teaspoon salt
10	tablespoons unsalted butter, softened but still firm (see figure 1, page 32)
1	cup minus 1 tablespoon granulated sugar
2	large eggs
1½	cups plain low-fat yogurt

INSTRUCTIONS:

1. Adjust oven rack to lower-middle position and heat oven to 375 degrees. Spray 12-hole muffin tin with vegetable cooking spray or coat lightly with butter.

2. Whisk flour, baking powder, baking soda, and salt together in medium bowl; set aside.

3. Cream butter and sugar with mixer on medium-high speed until light and fluffy, about 2 minutes. Add eggs, one at a time, beating well after each addition. Beat in one-half of dry ingredients. Beat in one-third of yogurt. Beat in remaining dry ingredients in two batches, alternating with yogurt, until incorporated. Divide batter evenly among holes in greased muffin tin (see figure 2, page 33).

4. Bake muffins until golden brown, 25 to 30 minutes. Set tin on wire rack to cool slightly, about 5 minutes. Remove muffins from tin and serve warm or at room temperature.

▪▪ **VARIATIONS:**

Mocha Chip Muffins

Follow master recipe, dissolving 3 tablespoons instant espresso powder in yogurt and folding 1 cup chocolate chips into finished batter.

Apricot Almond Muffins

Follow master recipe, creaming 1 ounce (3 tablespoons) almond paste with butter and sugar and folding 1½ cups finely diced dried apricots into finished batter. Sprinkle each batter top with portion of ½ cup sliced almonds.

Raspberry Almond Muffins

Follow master recipe, creaming 1 ounce (3 tablespoons) almond paste with butter and sugar. Spoon one-half portion of batter into each muffin cup. With small spoon, make well in center of each cup of dough. Spoon 1 to 1½ teaspoons raspberry (or any flavored) jam into each well. Fill with remaining batter. Sprinkle each batter top with portion of ½ cup sliced almonds.

Cranberry-Walnut-Orange Muffins

Follow master recipe, adding 2 teaspoons grated orange zest to butter and sugar mixture and folding 1½ cups coarsely chopped fresh or frozen cranberries and ¾ cup coarsely chopped walnuts into finished batter.

Lemon Blueberry Muffins

Follow master recipe, adding 2 teaspoons grated lemon zest to butter and sugar mixture and folding 1½ cups fresh or frozen (but not thawed) blueberries that have been tossed in 1 tablespoon flour into finished batter.

Lemon Poppy Seed Muffins

Follow master recipe, adding 3 tablespoons poppy seeds to dry ingredients and 1 tablespoon grated lemon zest to butter and sugar mixture. While muffins are baking, heat ¼ cup granulated sugar and ¼ cup lemon juice in small saucepan until sugar dissolves and mixture forms light syrup, 3 to 4 minutes. Brush warm syrup over muffins as soon as they come out of the oven. Cool and serve as directed.

Banana Walnut Muffins

Follow master recipe, adding ½ teaspoon grated nutmeg to dry ingredients, substituting 1 cup packed light brown sugar for granulated sugar, and folding 1½ cups finely diced ripe bananas (about 3 small) and ¾ cup chopped walnuts into finished batter.

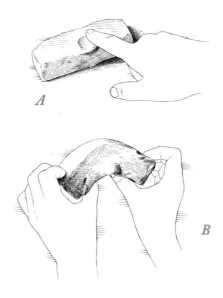

Figure 1.

Before creaming, butter must be brought to cool room temperature (about 67 degrees) so that it is malleable but not soft. Don't hurry this step. Cold butter can't hold as much air as properly softened butter, and the resulting muffins and quick breads may be too dense. If you don't have an instant-read thermometer to take the temperature of the butter, use these visual clues: (A) The butter should give slightly when pressed but still hold its shape. (B) The butter should bend with little resistance and without cracking or breaking.

Figure 2.
Use an ice cream scoop to portion batter into a muffin tin.

chapter three

BRAN MUFFINS

OST ANY MUFFIN CAN BE MADE AS A variation on our recipe for basic muffins in chapter 2. Bran muffins, however, require a different formula. While most muffins have a buttery, delicate yellow crumb, bran muffins should be dark, rich, hearty, and moist.

There are two basic types of bran muffins—so-called refrigerator muffins and muffins based on a classic batter. The batter for refrigerator muffins, which contains bran cereal, is simply mixed and then stored in the refrigerator until the cereal softens and becomes part of the batter. The "classic" batter muffins can be made by combining

34

ingredients according to the creaming method or the quick bread method (both explained on pages 17–18). Wheat bran, rather than cereal, is the most common source of bran in classic bran muffin recipes.

We conducted a bake-off, and the inferiority of the cereal-based refrigerator muffins was immediately obvious. They had a muddy look, a somewhat rubbery texture, and an oddly chewy quality. The bran flavor was dull and muted, and they lacked the all-around depth we expected from a bran muffin. By contrast, the classic bran muffins tasted deeply of bran and had a better (although still far from perfect) texture. Of the two approaches to making classic muffins, we preferred the creaming method (just as we did in our recipe for basic muffins) for its ability to create a fuller, more tender muffin.

With the mixing method decided, we moved on to the ingredients. A standard muffin batter is composed of flour, sugar, leavening, eggs, flavorings, milk, and fat. The batter's volume is built on a higher proportion of flour relative to fat and liquid. But when you reduce a portion of the flour to accommodate the bran, you disrupt the balance of liquid and dry ingredients, because wheat bran isn't actually absorbed into the batter the way flour is. This means that you need to rework the proportion of liquid and dry ingredients.

To understand this dynamic, it is important to know a

bit about bran. Bran, the exterior covering of wheat kernels, is milled into flakes. These flakes, known as wheat bran, are high in insoluble fiber. As a result, they are actually suspended in the batter, making a denser muffin. The bran flakes also tend to dry out and "break up" the batter, in much the same way that chocolate chips or nuts break up the batter in cookies.

When we started baking the muffins, we used a whopping two cups of bran. You can probably imagine the result: dry, crumbly muffins that tasted (and acted) just like sawdust. After much fine-tuning, we found that we could achieve a fuller, more tempered flavor and a more pleasing texture by replacing a little of the all-purpose flour with whole wheat flour. This allowed us to cut the bran down to 1½ cups without sacrificing the flavor we wanted.

Finally, we noticed that bran muffins tend to overbake in a flash. A tray of muffins are baked through when they retract ever so slightly from the sides of the cups and the tops spring back very gently on being touched. Don't look for an active spring. The muffins will be baked through even if a wooden pick withdrawn from the centers has a few moist crumbs clinging to it.

☙

Master Recipe

Bran Muffins
makes 1 dozen muffins

☞ **NOTE:** *Wheat bran is available at health foods stores. It is also available in supermarkets in boxes labeled Quaker Unprocessed Bran.*

	Vegetable cooking spray or unsalted butter for greasing muffin tin
1¼	cups all-purpose flour
¼	cup whole wheat flour
2	teaspoons baking powder
½	teaspoon baking soda
¾	teaspoon salt
1¼	teaspoons ground cinnamon
¾	teaspoon ground allspice
½	teaspoon freshly grated nutmeg
7	tablespoons unsalted butter, softened but still firm (see figure 1, page 32)
½	cup plus 2 tablespoons packed dark brown sugar
2	large eggs
2½	teaspoons vanilla extract

(ingredients continued on next page)

(ingredients continued from previous page)

3	tablespoons unsulphured molasses
¼	cup sour cream
1	cup plus 3 tablespoons buttermilk
1½	cups wheat bran
1	cup raisins

▪▪ INSTRUCTIONS:

1. Adjust oven rack to lower-middle position and heat oven to 375 degrees. Spray 12-hole muffin tin with vegetable cooking spray or coat lightly with butter.

2. Whisk flours, baking powder, baking soda, salt, and spices together in medium bowl; set aside.

3. Cream butter with mixer on medium speed until light and fluffy, 1 to 2 minutes. Add brown sugar, increase speed to medium-high, and beat until combined and fluffy, about 1 minute longer. Add eggs one at a time, beating well after each addition. Beat in vanilla, molasses, and sour cream until thoroughly combined and creamy, about 1 minute longer. Reduce speed to low; beat in buttermilk and half the flour mixture until combined, about 1 minute. Beat in remaining flour mixture until incorporated and slightly curdled looking, about 1 minute longer, scraping sides of bowl as necessary. Stir in bran and raisins. Divide batter evenly among holes in greased muffin tin (see figure 2, page 33).

4. Bake until a toothpick inserted into muffin center withdraws cleanly or with a few moist particles adhering to it, about 25 minutes. Set tin on wire rack to cool slightly, about 5 minutes. Remove muffins from tin and serve warm or at room temperature.

chapter four

BUTTERMILK BISCUITS

BISCUITS SHARE WITH MUFFINS THE DISTINC-
tion of being among the simplest of all breads.
They are made from a mixture of flour, leavener (baking powder or soda), salt, fat (usually
butter or vegetable shortening), and liquid (milk, buttermilk, sour milk, yogurt, or cream). To make them, one cuts
fat into the dry ingredients, as when making pie dough; the
liquid is then stirred in until a dough forms. Biscuits are
usually rolled out and cut, although they can also be shaped
by hand or dropped onto a baking sheet by the spoonful.

We began our testing by focusing on the flour. We found
that the kind of flour you choose has a great effect on the bis-

cuit you end up with. The main factor here is the proportion of protein in the flour. Low-protein, or "soft," flour (such as cake flour or White Lily, a favored brand in the South) encourages a tender, cakelike texture as well as a more moist crumb. Higher-protein, or "strong," flour (such as all-purpose flour) promotes a crispier crust and a drier, denser crumb.

Tasters liked the crispier crust of the biscuits made with all-purpose flour and the tender, airy crumb of the biscuits made with cake flour. We found that a combination of half cake flour and half all-purpose flour delivered the best results—a crisp crust and a tender crumb. If you don't have cake flour, all-purpose flour makes a fine biscuit as long as you add more liquid to the batter.

Fat makes biscuits (and other pastries) tender, moist, smooth, and tasty. Butter, of course, delivers the best flavor, while vegetable shortening makes a slightly flakier biscuit with better holding powers. However, we don't think this gain in shelf life is worth the loss in flavor. Stick with unsalted butter when making biscuits.

We discovered that a proportion of ½ cup fat to 2 cups flour provides the best balance of tenderness and richness with structure. If you use less fat, your biscuits will rise well, but they will be tough and dry. If you use more, your biscuits will have a lovely texture but they may end up a bit squat.

After mixing flour and leavening, you must "rub" the fat

into the dry ingredients, making a dry, coarse mixture akin to large bread crumbs or rolled oats, with some slightly bigger lumps mixed in. This rubbing may seem unimportant, but in fact it is crucial to the proper rising of the biscuits. Gas released by the leavening during baking must have a space in which to collect; if the texture of the dough is homogeneous, the gas will simply dissipate. Melting fat particles create convenient spaces in which the gas can collect, form a bubble, and produce a rise. Proper rubbing breaks the fat into tiny bits and disperses it throughout the dough. As the fat melts during baking, its place is taken up by gas and steam, which expand and push the dough up. The wider the dispersal of the fat, the more even the rising of the dough.

If, however, the fat softens and binds with the dry ingredients during rubbing, it forms a pasty goo, the spaces collapse, and the biscuits become leaden. To produce light, airy biscuits, the fat must remain cold and firm, which means rubbing must be deft and quick. Traditionally, biscuit makers pinch the cut-up fat into the dry ingredients, using only their fingertips—never the whole hand, which is too warm—and they pinch hard and fast, practically flinging the little bits of flour and fat into the bowl after each pinch. Less experienced cooks sometimes cut in the fat by scraping two knives in opposite directions or by using a bow-shaped pastry blender. We found, however, that there is no reason not to use the food processor for this task: pulsing the dry ingredients and the fat is fast and almost foolproof.

After cutting in the fat, liquid is added and the dough is stirred, just until the ingredients are bound, using a light hand so the gluten will not become activated. We found that buttermilk (or plain yogurt) gives biscuits the best flavor. It also creates a lighter, airier texture than regular milk. That's because the acid in the buttermilk reacts with the leaveners to increase the rise.

Biscuits are best formed by gently patting gobs of dough between your hands. If the work surface, the dough, and the cutter are generously floured, fluffy biscuits can be rolled and cut; but the softness of the dough makes this a tricky procedure, and the extra flour and handling will make the biscuits heavier and somewhat dense.

Because they need quick heat, biscuits are best baked in the middle of the oven. Placed too close to the bottom, they burn on the underside and remain pale on top; set too near the oven roof, they do not rise well because the outside hardens into a shell before the inside has had a chance to rise properly. As soon as they are light brown, they are done. Be careful, as overcooking will dry them out. Biscuits are always at their best when served as soon as they come out of the oven. The dough, however, may be made some hours in advance and baked when needed; the biscuits will still rise well.

ᴟ

Master Recipe

Buttermilk Biscuits
makes 12

➤ **NOTE:** *Mixing the butter and dry ingredients quickly so the butter remains cold and firm is crucial to producing light, tender biscuits. The easiest and most reliable approach is to use a food processor fitted with a steel blade. Expect a soft and slightly sticky dough. The wet dough creates steam when the biscuits bake and promotes the light airy texture. If the dough is too wet for you to shape the biscuits by hand, lightly flour your hands and then shape the biscuits.*

1	cup all-purpose flour
1	cup plain cake flour
2	teaspoons baking powder
½	teaspoon baking soda
1	teaspoon sugar
½	teaspoon salt
8	tablespoons chilled unsalted butter, cut into ¼-inch cubes (see figures 3 through 5, pages 47–48)
¾	cup cold buttermilk, or ¾ cup plus 2 tablespoons plain yogurt

⁝ INSTRUCTIONS:

1. Adjust oven rack to middle position and heat oven to 450 degrees.

2. Place flours, baking powder, baking soda, sugar, and salt in large bowl or workbowl of a food processor fitted with steel blade. Whisk together or pulse six times.

3. If making by hand, use two knives, a pastry blender, or your fingertips to quickly cut in butter until mixture resembles coarse meal with a few slightly larger butter lumps. If using food processor, remove cover and distribute butter evenly over dry ingredients. Cover and pulse 12 times, each pulse lasting 1 second.

4. If making by hand, stir in buttermilk with a rubber spatula or fork until mixture forms soft, slightly sticky ball. If using food processor, remove cover and pour buttermilk evenly over dough. Pulse until dough gathers into moist clumps, about eight 1-second pulses.

5. Transfer dough to a lightly floured surface and quickly form into rough ball. Be careful not to overmix. Using a sharp knife or dough cutter, divide dough in quarters and then cut each quarter into thirds. Quickly and gently shape each piece into a rough ball (see figure 6, page 49), and place on ungreased cookie sheet. (Baking sheet can be wrapped in plastic and refrigerated for up to 2 hours.)

6. Bake until biscuit tops are light brown, 10 to 12 minutes. Serve immediately.

⁞⁞ VARIATIONS:

Buttermilk Biscuits with All-Purpose Flour

We find that a blend of cake flour and all-purpose flour creates a light, airy, and tender biscuit. If you don't have cake flour on hand, you can use all-purpose flour alone, although the crumb will be coarser and the crust crispier because of the higher protein content in the flour.

Follow master recipe, replacing cake flour with an extra cup of all-purpose flour. Increase buttermilk or yogurt by 2 tablespoons.

Sweet Milk Biscuits

Buttermilk (or yogurt) adds richness and a distinctive tang to the biscuits while also helping the dough to rise. Biscuits made with whole milk are not as flavorful and need extra baking powder to rise properly.

Follow master recipe, replacing buttermilk with ¾ cup whole milk and increasing baking powder to 1 tablespoon.

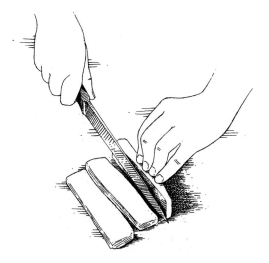

Figure 3.
Cut the butter lengthwise into three even strips.

Figure 4.
Separate the strips and then cut each lengthwise into thirds.

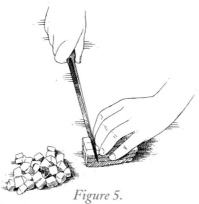

Figure 5.
Stack the strips on top of each other, then cut them crosswise
into ¼-inch dice.

Figure 6.

*Our buttermilk biscuit dough is too soft to roll and cut. Using a
sharp knife or dough cutter, divide dough in quarters and then
cut each quarter into thirds. With lightly cupped hands, gently
shape each piece into a ball.*

chapter five

CREAM BISCUITS

OUR BUTTERMILK BISCUITS (SEE CHAPTER 4) are easy to prepare: You can have biscuits on the table in 20 minutes. But many cooks are intimidated by this kind of biscuit because they are not comfortable with the traditional process of cutting butter into flour.

We wondered if we could come up with a great recipe for homemade biscuits that can be made quickly and easily and that does not require cutting fat into flour. In short, was it possible to take the guesswork out of making biscuits to create a foolproof recipe?

We began with a basic recipe calling for 2 cups flour, 2

teaspoons baking powder, 1 tablespoon sugar, and ½ teaspoon salt. Now we had to figure out what to add to this mixture instead of butter or vegetable shortening to make a dough. We decided to try plain yogurt, sour cream, milk, milk combined with melted butter, and whipped heavy cream, an idea we borrowed from a scone recipe.

The biscuits made with yogurt and sour cream were a bit sodden in texture, those with the milk and milk/butter combination were tough and lifeless, and the whipped cream biscuit was too light, more confection than biscuit. This last approach also required another step—whipping the cream—which seemed like too much trouble for a simple recipe. So we tried using plain heavy cream, without whipping, and this biscuit was the best of the lot. (Cream biscuits are not our invention. James Beard includes such a recipe in his seminal work *American Cookery* [Little, Brown, 1972].)

Next, we decided to do a blind tasting, pitting the cream biscuits against our conventional buttermilk biscuit recipe, which requires cutting butter into the flour. The result? Both biscuits had their partisans. The cream biscuits were lighter and more tender. They were also richer tasting. The buttermilk biscuits were flakier and had the distinctive tang that many tasters associate with good biscuits. Although neither biscuit was sweet, the buttermilk version seemed more savory.

At this point, we decided that cream biscuits were a worthy (and easier) alternative to traditional buttermilk biscuits. Still, we were running into a problem with the shape of the biscuits, which spread far too much during baking. We have always followed the conventional advice about not overworking the dough. In our experience, the best biscuits are generally made from dough that is handled lightly. This is certainly true of buttermilk biscuits.

But cream biscuits, being less sturdy than those made with butter, become soft and "melt" during baking. In this case, we thought, a little handling might not be such a bad thing.

So we baked up two batches: The first dough we patted out gingerly; the second dough we kneaded for 30 seconds until it was smooth and uniform in appearance. The results were remarkable. The more heavily worked dough produced much higher, fluffier biscuits than the lightly handled dough, which looked short and bedraggled.

We ran into a problem, however, when one batch of biscuits had to sit for a few minutes while we waited for the oven to heat up. During baking, the dough spread, resulting in biscuits with bottoms that were too wide and tops that were too narrow. Clearly, the biscuits had to be popped into the oven immediately after cutting. As for dough thickness, ¾ inch provides a remarkably high rise, more appealing than biscuits that start out ½ inch thick. We also discovered that it was best to add just enough cream to hold the dough together. A wet dough does not hold its shape as well during baking.

Although we find it easy enough to quickly roll out this dough and then cut it into rounds with a biscuit cutter, you can simply shape the dough with your hands or push it into the bottom of an 8-inch cake pan. The dough can then be flipped onto the work surface and cut into wedges with a knife or dough scraper.

We also tested making drop biscuits, a method in which the dough is simply scooped up and dropped onto a baking sheet. These biscuits did not rise very well and their shape was inferior. It was also more time-consuming to drop the batter in individual spoonfuls than to simply shape the dough in one piece.

Our final ingredient tests involved sugar—the tasters felt that 1 tablespoon was a bit much, so we dropped it to 2 teaspoons—and baking powder, which we found we could reduce to 1 teaspoon with no decrease in rise. For oven temperature, we tried 375, 400, and 425 degrees, and the latter was best for browning.

Now we had the simplest of biscuit recipes: Whisk together the flour, sugar, baking powder, and salt in a medium bowl, add 1½ cups of heavy cream, form the dough, knead it for 30 seconds, cut it, and bake for 15 minutes at 425 degrees. The results will surprise you.

Master Recipe

Cream Biscuits
makes 8

➤ NOTE: *This recipe provides the quickest and easiest way to make biscuits. Bake the biscuits immediately after cutting them; letting them stand for any length of time can decrease the leavening power and thereby prevent the biscuits from rising properly in the oven.*

2	cups all-purpose flour
2	teaspoons sugar
1	teaspoon baking powder
½	teaspoon salt
1½	cups heavy cream

∷ INSTRUCTIONS:

1. Adjust oven rack to upper-middle position and heat oven to 425 degrees. Line baking sheet with parchment paper.

2. Whisk together flour, sugar, baking powder, and salt in medium bowl. Add 1¼ cups cream and stir with wooden spoon until dough forms, about 30 seconds. Transfer dough from bowl to countertop, leaving all dry, floury bits behind in bowl. In 1 tablespoon increments, add up to ¼ cup cream to dry bits in bowl, mixing with wooden spoon after each

54

addition, until moistened. Add these moistened bits to rest of dough and knead by hand just until smooth, about 30 seconds.

3. Following figures 7 through 10 (pages 56–57), cut biscuits into rounds or wedges. Place rounds or wedges on parchment-lined baking sheet and bake until golden brown, about 15 minutes. Serve immediately.

VARIATIONS:

Cream Biscuits with Fresh Herbs
Use the herb of your choice in this variation.

Follow master recipe, whisking 2 tablespoons minced fresh herbs into flour along with sugar, baking powder, and salt.

Cream Biscuits with Cheddar Cheese
Follow master recipe, stirring ½ cup (2 ounces) sharp cheddar cheese cut into ¼-inch pieces into flour along with sugar, baking powder, and salt. Increase baking time to 18 minutes.

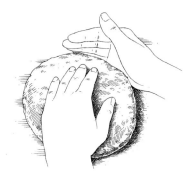

Figure 7.
For round biscuits, pat the dough on a lightly floured work
surface into a ¾-inch-thick circle.

Figure 8.
Punch out the dough rounds with a biscuit cutter. Push together
the remaining pieces of dough, pat into a ¾-inch-thick round, and
punch out several more biscuits. Discard the remaining scraps.

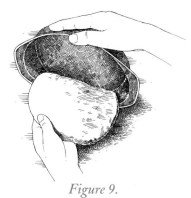

Figure 9.
To make wedges, press the dough into an 8-inch cake pan, then
turn the dough out onto a lightly floured work surface.

Figure 10.
With a knife or bench scraper, cut the dough into 8 wedges.

chapter six

SCONES

SCONES, THE QUINTESSENTIAL TEA CAKE OF THE British Isles, were intended to be delicate, fluffy biscuits, which may come as a surprise to Americans. The clunky mounds of oven-baked sweetened dough that the British call rock cakes are often called scones in our restaurants and coffee shops. Unlike rock cakes, in which dough is dropped from a spoon onto a baking sheet, traditional scones are quickly rolled or patted out and cut into rounds or wedges.

We began our testing with the flour. We constructed a composite recipe and then made one version with bread flour, one with all-purpose flour, and another with cake flour. The differences in outcome were astonishing. The scones made with bread flour were heavy and tough. Those made with all-purpose flour were lighter and much more flavorful. Cake flour produced scones that were doughy in the center, with a raw taste and poor texture.

With the question of flour type easily settled, we experimented with fat in the form of butter and then lard. We decided we preferred the rich flavor of butter. (Although lard is not used much in home baking anymore, we can understand why commercial bakers might prefer it. Day-old scones made with lard hold up better than those made with butter. The preservative effects of different fats, along with lower cost, may be why store-bought scones are often made with margarine or other hydrogenated fats.) Although the amount of solid fat can be varied, we found 5 tablespoons butter to 2 cups flour to be just right. More butter and the scones almost melted in the oven, less butter and they turned out dry and tough.

The choice of liquid can also profoundly affect the flavor of a scone. We tested various liquids and found that cream made the best scones that were tender yet still light. Scones made with milk were bland and dry. Buttermilk gave us scones with plenty of flavor, but they were also too flaky and biscuitlike. Scones made with cream were more moist and flavorful than the others.

We tried adding an egg to the dough and found that this made the scones very cakey, more American (or rocklike) in style than British. Many tasters liked the effect of the egg, however, and because it helps the scone hold onto moisture and remain fresh tasting longer, we decided to use the egg in a variation on our master recipe called Cakey Scones.

In traditional recipes, one to two tablespoons of sugar is enough to sweeten an entire batch of scones. American scones tend to be far sweeter than the British versions, which are usually sweetened with toppings such as jam. Americans seem to eat their scones the way they eat their muffins, without anything more than a smear of butter, so the sweetness is baked in. We prefer the British approach, but to accommodate American tastes we decided to increase the sugar slightly to three tablespoons.

Finally, scones are often glazed to enhance their appearance and add sweetness. We tried brushing the dough with a beaten egg as well as with heavy cream just before baking. Scones brushed with egg became too dark in the oven. We preferred the more delicate look of scones brushed with cream and then dusted with a little granulated sugar.

Scones can be mixed by hand or with a food processor. (The processor is used to cut fat into flour; minimal hand mixing is required afterward.) As with biscuits, we found the food processor to be more reliable than hand mixing, which can overheat the butter and cause it to soften. The same shaping technique used with wedge-shaped biscuits works perfectly with scones, even though this dough is a bit stickier. Just pat the dough into a cake pan, gently pop it out onto a floured surface, and then cut the dough into eight wedges.

👑

Master Recipe

Cream Scones

makes 8

➤ **NOTE:** *The traditional British scone is somewhat sweet and biscuitlike in texture. If you prefer a more cakelike texture, or want the scones to stay fresh tasting longer, try the Cakey Scones variation. As with buttermilk biscuits, the easiest and most reliable approach to mixing the butter into the dry ingredients is to use a food processor fitted with a steel blade. Resist the urge to eat the scones hot out of the oven. Letting them cool for at least 10 minutes firms them up and improves their texture.*

2	cups all-purpose flour
1	tablespoon baking powder
3	tablespoons sugar
½	teaspoon salt
5	tablespoons chilled unsalted butter, cut into ¼-inch cubes (see figures 3 through 5, pages 47–48)
½	cup currants
1	cup heavy cream

⠿ INSTRUCTIONS:

1. Adjust oven rack to middle position and heat oven to 425 degrees.

2. Place flour, baking powder, sugar, and salt in large bowl or workbowl of a food processor fitted with steel blade. Whisk together or pulse 6 times.

3. If making by hand, use two knives, a pastry blender, or your fingertips and quickly cut in butter until mixture resembles coarse meal with a few slightly larger butter lumps. If using food processor, remove cover and distribute butter evenly over dry ingredients. Cover and pulse 12 times, each pulse lasting 1 second. Add currants and quickly mix in or pulse one more time.

4. If making by hand, stir in heavy cream with rubber spatula or fork until dough begins to form, about 30 seconds. If using food processor, remove cover and pour cream evenly over dough. Pulse until dough just starts to gather into moist, pebblelike clumps, eight to ten 1-second pulses.

5. Transfer dough and all dry floury bits to countertop and knead dough by hand just until it comes together into a rough, slightly sticky ball, 5 to 10 seconds. Following figures 9 and 10 on page 57, cut scones into 8 wedges. Place wedges on ungreased cookie sheet. (Baking sheet can be wrapped in plastic and refrigerated for up to 2 hours.)

6. Bake until scone tops are light brown, 12 to 15 minutes. Cool on wire rack for at least 10 minutes. Serve warm or at room temperature.

■■ VARIATIONS:

Glazed Scones

A light glaze of cream and sugar gives scones an attractive sheen and sweeter flavor. If baking scones immediately after making the dough, glaze dough just before cutting it into wedges. If scones have been held in the refrigerator, apply the glaze to each wedge.

Follow master recipe, brushing tops of scones with 1 tablespoon heavy cream and then sprinkling with 1 tablespoon sugar just before baking them.

Cakey Scones

An egg changes the texture and color of the scones and helps to preserve freshness. You can keep them up to 2 days in an airtight container.

Follow master recipe, reducing butter to 4 tablespoons and cream to ¾ cup. Add 1 large egg, lightly beaten, to dough along with cream.

Oatmeal Raisin Scones

We found that old-fashioned rolled oats produced the best oatmeal scones, with a flakier texture and more noticeable oat flavor than quick-cooking oats. Mix this dough in the food processor; the pulsing action of the blade breaks down the coarse oats and incorporates them into the dough.

Follow master recipe, making dough in food processor

and substituting 1 cup rolled oats for ½ cup all-purpose flour. Replace currants with ¾ cup raisins. Increase sugar to 4 tablespoons and butter to 6 tablespoons.

Ginger Scones

Follow master recipe, substituting ½ cup chopped crystallized ginger for currants.

Cranberry Orange Scones

Follow master recipe, adding 1 teaspoon grated orange zest with butter and substituting ¾ cup dried cranberries for currants.

Lemon Blueberry Scones

Mix the dough by hand after adding the blueberries to keep the blueberries plump and whole.

Follow master recipe, adding 1 teaspoon grated lemon zest with butter and substituting ½ cup fresh or frozen (do not thaw) blueberries for currants.

chapter seven

CORNBREAD & CORN MUFFINS

WHILE ALL CORNBREADS ARE QUICK TO make and bake, there are two very distinct types: northern and southern. Southerners use 100 percent white cornmeal, and they like their cornbread crumbly, dry, and flat. Most northerners prefer sweeter, lighter, and higher golden cornbreads, which they achieve by adding sugar and combining white flour and yellow cornmeal. Both types of cornbread sport a brown crust, although southern cornbread crusts are also crisp and crunchy.

After an initial round of testing, we realized that we preferred something in between, with elements of both styles incorporated into a single recipe. We liked the pure corn flavor of southern cornbread but wanted a crumb that was more moist and tender. Northern cornbread was more tender but was also fluffy, and the corn flavor was muted. We decided to start out with a southern-style recipe, since it had more of the elements that we liked.

The type of cornmeal was a natural place to begin our testing. We tested 11 different cornmeals in a simple southern cornbread recipe. Before these tests, we would have bet that color was a regional idiosyncrasy that had little to do with flavor. But tasting proved otherwise. Cornbreads made with yellow cornmeal consistently had a more potent corn flavor than those made with white meal.

How the cornmeal was ground also affected flavor. Large commercial mills use huge steel rollers to grind dent corn (a hard, dry corn) into cornmeal. This is how Quaker, the leading supermarket brand, is produced. But some smaller mills scattered across the United States grind with millstones; this product is called stone-ground cornmeal. (If water is used as an energy source, the cornmeal may be labeled "water-ground.") Stone-ground cornmeal is usually a bit coarser than cornmeal processed through steel rollers.

These smaller millers may also choose not to degerm, or remove all of the germ, cleanly from the kernel, as commercial mills do. This makes their product closer to a whole-grain cornmeal. If the color is uniform, the germ has been removed. A stone-ground cornmeal with some germ will have flecks that are both lighter and darker than the predominant color, whether that's yellow or white.

In our tests, we found the texture of cornbreads made with stone-ground meals to be more interesting, since the cornmeals were not of a uniform grind. More important, we found that cornbreads made with stone-ground cornmeal tasted much better than those made with the standard Quaker cornmeal.

The higher moisture and oil content of stone-ground cornmeal causes it to go rancid within weeks. If you buy some, wrap it tightly in plastic, or put it into a moisture-proof container, then refrigerate or freeze it. Degerminated cornmeals, such as Quaker, keep for a year if stored in a dry, cool place.

We were set on the cornmeal—yellow, preferably stone-ground. The next issue was flour. For cornbread with a rich corn flavor, we found that flour is best omitted. (For corn muffins, some flour is necessary; see page 74.)

Although we didn't want cornbread to taste like dessert, we wondered whether a little sugar might enhance the corn flavor. So we made three batches—one with no sugar, one with two teaspoons, and one with a heaping tablespoon. The higher-sugar bread was really too sweet for our tastes, but two teaspoons of sugar seemed to enhance the natural sweetness of the corn without calling attention to itself.

So far all of our testing had been done with a composite recipe under which most southern cornbread recipes seemed to fall. We had, however, run across a recipe that didn't quite fit the mold, and now seemed like the right time to give it a try.

In this simple version, boiling water is stirred into the cornmeal, then modest amounts of milk, egg, butter, salt, and baking powder are stirred into the resulting cornmeal mush and the whole thing is baked. So simple, so lean, so humble, so backwater, this recipe would have been easy to pass over. Just one bite completely changed the direction of our pursuit. Unlike anything we had tasted so far, the crumb of this cornbread was incredibly moist and fine and bursting with corn flavor, all with no flour and virtually no fat.

We were pleased, but since the foundation of this bread was cornmeal mush, the crumb was actually more mushy than moist. In addition, the baking powder, the only dry ingredient left, got stirred into the wet batter at the end. This just didn't feel right.

After a few unsuccessful attempts to make this cornbread less mushy, we started thinking that this great idea was a bust. In a last attempt to salvage it, we decided to make mush out of only half the cornmeal and to mix the remaining cornmeal with the leavener. To our relief, the bread made this way was much improved. Decreasing the mush even further—from a half to a third of the corn-meal—gave us exactly what we were looking for. We made the new, improved cornbread with buttermilk and mixed a bit of baking soda with the baking powder, and it tasted even better. Finally, our recipe was starting to feel right.

With this new recipe in hand, we performed a few more tests. We tried vegetable oil, peanut oil, shortening, butter, and bacon drippings. Butter and bacon drippings were pleasant flavor additions and improved the texture of the cornbread by making it less crumbly.

Before conducting these cornbread tests, we didn't think it was possible to bake cornbread in too hot an oven, but after tasting breads baked on the bottom rack of a 475-degree oven, we found that a dark brown crust makes bitter bread. We moved the rack up a notch, reduced the oven temperature to 450 degrees, and were thus able to cook many loaves of cornbread to golden brown perfection.

One final question: Do you need to heat up the skillet before adding the batter? If you're not a southerner, the answer is no. Although the bread will not be as crisp in an unheated pan, it will ultimately brown up with a longer baking time. If you are a southerner, of course, the answer is yes. More than the color of the meal or the presence of sugar or flour, what makes cornbread southern is the batter hitting the hot fat in a cast-iron skillet.

⚜️

Master Recipe

Cornbread
serves 8

➤ **N O T E :** *This cornbread is thin and crusty, making it the perfect accompaniment to soups, chili, or stews. Make sure that the water is at a rapid boil when it is added to the cornmeal. If you prefer a sweeter, more northern-style recipe, see the note to the corn muffin recipe on page 74.*

4	teaspoons bacon drippings or 1 teaspoon vegetable oil plus 1 tablespoon unsalted butter, melted
1	cup yellow cornmeal, preferably stone-ground
2	teaspoons sugar
½	teaspoon salt
1	teaspoon baking powder
¼	teaspoon baking soda
½	cup rapidly boiling water
¾	cup buttermilk
1	large egg, beaten lightly

░ **I N S T R U C T I O N S :**

1. Adjust oven rack to lower-middle position and heat oven to 450 degrees. Set 8-inch cast-iron skillet with bacon fat (or vegetable oil) in heating oven.

2. Measure ⅓ cup cornmeal into medium bowl. Whisk remaining cornmeal, sugar, salt, baking powder, and baking soda together in small bowl; set aside.

3. Pour ¼ cup boiling water all at once into the ⅓ cup cornmeal; whisk quickly to combine. Continue adding water, a tablespoon at a time, until mixtures forms thick mush (see figure 11, page 73). Whisk in buttermilk gradually, breaking up lumps until smooth, then whisk in egg. When oven is preheated and skillet very hot, stir dry ingredients into mush mixture until just moistened. Carefully remove skillet from oven. If using bacon fat, pour it from pan into batter and stir to incorporate. If pan has been greased with vegetable oil, stir melted butter into batter.

4. Quickly pour batter into heated skillet. Bake until golden brown, about 20 minutes. Remove from oven and instantly turn cornbread onto wire rack; cool for 5 minutes. Serve warm or at room temperature.

▪▪ VARIATIONS:

Cornbread with Chiles

Follow master recipe, folding in 1 to 2 medium jalapeño chiles, seeded and minced, after bacon fat or melted butter has been incorporated.

Cornbread with Cheddar Cheese
Follow master recipe, folding in 2 ounces (½ cup) shredded cheddar cheese after bacon fat or melted butter has been incorporated.

Cornbread with Corn Kernels
Follow master recipe, folding in ¾ cup fresh or frozen corn kernels after bacon fat or melted butter has been incorporated.

Figure 11.
The cornmeal mush must have just the right texture. The batter should neither clump together nor be too thin. Ideally, the mush will be soft, like polenta. The consistency will be thick enough to give the batter body but pliable enough to accommodate wet ingredients easily.

Corn Muffins
makes 12

➤ NOTE: *Adding more sugar, another egg, and some cake flour turns cornbread into muffins. The flour and egg help create a cakier (less crumbly) texture, while the sugar makes the muffins seem less savory. This batter is fairly thin; if you like, transfer the batter to a 1-quart measuring cup and pour it into the greased muffin tin. If you like a cakier, sweet cornbread, like those made in the North, bake this batter in a greased 8-inch cast-iron skillet or square pan for 25 minutes.*

	Vegetable cooking spray or unsalted butter for greasing muffin tin
1¾	cups yellow cornmeal, preferably stone-ground
½	cup cake flour
½	cup sugar
¾	teaspoon salt
2	teaspoons baking powder
½	teaspoon baking soda
¾	cup rapidly boiling water
1¼	cups buttermilk
2	large eggs, beaten lightly
2	tablespoons unsalted butter, melted

INSTRUCTIONS:

1. Adjust oven rack to lower-middle position and heat oven to 425 degrees. Spray 12-hole muffin tin with vegetable cooking spray or coat lightly with butter.

2. Measure ½ cup cornmeal into medium bowl. Whisk remaining cornmeal, flour, sugar, salt, baking powder, and baking soda together in small bowl; set aside.

3. Pour ⅓ cup boiling water all at once into the ½ cup cornmeal; whisk quickly to combine. Continue adding water, a tablespoon at a time, until mixtures forms thick mush (see figure 11, page 73). Whisk in buttermilk gradually, breaking up lumps until smooth, then whisk in eggs. Stir dry ingredients into mush mixture until just moistened. Stir in melted butter just until incorporated. Ladle batter into greased muffin tin, filling holes almost to rim.

4. Bake until muffins are golden brown, 18 to 20 minutes. Set tin on wire rack to cool slightly, about 5 minutes. Remove muffins from tin and serve warm or at room temperature.

chapter eight

IRISH SODA BREAD

RICH, SWEET AMERICAN-STYLE IRISH SODA bread is filled with raisins and caraway seeds. It is delicious, but its uses are limited to breakfast or snacking. Authentic Irish soda bread has a tender, dense crumb and a rough-textured, crunchy crust. It is versatile enough to be served with butter and jam at breakfast, for sandwiches at lunch, or alongside the evening meal. We set out to devise a recipe for this leaner, more savory style of soda bread.

As we looked over a multitude of recipes for soda bread, we found that they fell into two categories. The American versions contained eggs, butter, and sugar in varying amounts, along with caraway seeds, raisins, and a multitude of other flavorings. But most Irish cookbooks combined only four ingredients: flour (white and/or whole wheat), baking soda, salt, and buttermilk.

Flour, being the predominant ingredient, seemed like a good place to start our investigative baking. Because of Ireland's climate, the wheat grown there is a "soft," or low-protein, variety. While not suitable for strong European-style yeast breads, this flour is perfect for chemically leavened breads. This is basically because flour with a lower protein content produces a finer crumb and more tender product, key for breads that don't have the light texture provided when yeast is used as the leavener.

After suffering through several tough, heavy loaves made with unbleached all-purpose flour, we started exploring different proportions of cake flour and all-purpose flour. And, in fact, the bread did become more tender and a little lighter with the addition of some cake flour. As the ratio of cake to all-purpose exceeded 1:1, however, the bread became much more compact and heavy, with an undesirable mouthfeel— 1 cup of cake flour to 3 cups of all-purpose proved best.

Because the liquid-to-dry ratio is important in determining texture and moistness, we decided to test buttermilk next. As it turned out, bread made with 1¾ or 1⅔ cups of buttermilk produced bread that was doughy, almost gummy. With 1½ cups, the dough was firmer yet still moist, and the resulting bread was no longer doughy. (If you don't have buttermilk on hand, plain yogurt can be substituted for an equally delicious bread with a slightly rougher crust and lighter texture.)

With the amount of buttermilk decided upon, we were now ready to explore the amount and type of leavening to use. After trying various combinations of baking soda, baking powder, and cream of tartar, we found that 1½ teaspoons of soda, combined with an equal amount of cream of tartar, provided just the right amount of lift for a bread that should be light but not airy. Relying on cream of tartar (rather than the acidity in the buttermilk) to react with the baking soda allows the tangy buttermilk flavor to come through.

Because baking soda begins reacting immediately with the cream of tartar and does not provide the big second rise you get with double-acting baking powder, it is important to mix the dough quickly and not too vigorously. If you mix too slowly or too enthusiastically, too much carbon dioxide will be formed and will dissipate during the mixing process; not enough carbon dioxide will then be produced during baking to provide the proper rise. Extended kneading also overdevelops the gluten in the flour, toughening the bread.

Although we were making progress, the flavor of these basic loaves was mediocre at best, lacking depth and dimension, and they were also a bit tough. Traditionally, very small amounts of sugar and/or butter are sometimes added to soda bread, so, starting with sugar, we baked loaves with one and two tablespoons. Two tablespoons of sugar added just the flavor balance that was needed without making the bread sweet. It was only with the introduction of butter, though, that the loaves began to lose their toughness and become outstanding. Still, we really wanted to maintain the integrity of this basic bread and avoid making it too rich. After trying tests with one to four tablespoons of unsalted butter, two tablespoons proved a clear winner. This bread was tender but not crumbly, compact but not heavy. More than two tablespoons of butter began to shift the flavor balance of the bread and add unnecessary richness.

We were getting very close to our goal, but the crust was still too hard, thick, and crumbly. We wanted crunch, but crispness and tenderness as well.

In our research, we came upon various techniques for modifying the crust. Some dealt with the way the bread was baked, while others concentrated on how the bread was treated after baking. Trying to inhibit the formation of a thick crust by covering the bread with a bowl during the first 30 minutes of baking helped some, but the resulting bread took longer to bake and was paler and uneven in color. Using a large flowerpot and clay dish to simulate a cloche (a covered earthenware dish specifically designed for baking bread) again gave us a bread that didn't color well, even with both preheating the tray and buttering the dough.

But the next test, which, not coincidentally, closely simulated historical cooking methods for Irish soda bread, was a breakthrough. Baking the loaf in a well-buttered Dutch oven or cast-iron pot, covered only for the first 30 minutes, produced a well-risen loaf with an even, golden crust that was thin and crisp yet still had a bit of chew.

We realized, however, that not everyone has a cast-iron pot available, so we explored ways of softening the crust after baking. Wrapping the bread in a clean tea towel as soon as it emerged from the oven helped soften the crust, while a slightly damp tea towel softened it even more. The best technique, though, was to brush the warm loaf with some melted butter. This gave it an attractive sheen as well as a delicious, buttery crust with just enough crunch.

Although we liked the crust of the bread baked in the Dutch oven a little better, the ease of baking it on a baking sheet made the loaf brushed with butter a more practical option.

Finally, make sure that you cool the bread for at least 45 minutes before serving. If cut when too hot, the bread will be dense and slightly doughy.

♔

Master Recipe

Classic Irish Soda Bread
makes 1 loaf

➤ NOTE: *This bread is a great accompaniment to soups or stews, and leftovers make fine toast. With their flavorful grains and additions, the variations can stand alone.*

3	cups all-purpose flour
1	cup cake flour
2	tablespoons sugar
1½	teaspoons baking soda
1½	teaspoons cream of tartar
1½	teaspoons salt
2	tablespoons chilled unsalted butter, cut into ¼-inch cubes (see figures 3 through 5, pages 47–48), plus 1 tablespoon melted butter for crust
1½	cups buttermilk or plain yogurt

⁞ INSTRUCTIONS:

1. Adjust oven rack to upper-middle position and heat oven to 400 degrees. Whisk flours, sugar, baking soda, cream of tartar, and salt together in large bowl. Work diced butter into dry ingredients with fork or fingertips until texture resembles coarse crumbs.

2. Add buttermilk and stir with a fork just until dough begins to come together. Turn out onto lightly flour-coated work surface; knead until dough just becomes cohesive and bumpy, 12 to 14 turns. (Do not knead until dough is smooth, or bread will be tough.)

3. Pat dough into a round about 6 inches in diameter and 2½ inches high; place on greased or parchment-lined baking sheet. Score dough by cutting cross shape on top of loaf (see figure 12, page 83).

4. Bake until golden brown and a skewer inserted into center of loaf comes out clean or internal temperature reaches 180 degrees, 40 to 45 minutes. Remove from oven and brush with melted butter; cool for 45 minutes. Serve warm or at room temperature. Once cooled, bread can be wrapped in plastic and stored at room temperature for a couple of days.

▓ **VARIATIONS:**

Irish Brown Soda Bread

Unlike the Classic Irish Soda Bread dough, which is dry, this dough is extremely sticky.

Follow master recipe, making the following changes: Decrease all-purpose flour to 1¾ cups and cake flour to ½ cup. Add 1¼ cups stone-ground whole wheat flour and ½ cup toasted wheat germ to flour mixture. Replace granulated sugar with 3 tablespoons brown sugar. Bake bread to internal temperature of 190 degrees, 45 to 55 minutes.

American-Style Soda Bread with Raisins and Caraway
This dough is wet and sticky.

Follow master recipe, making the following changes: Increase sugar to ¼ cup and softened butter to 4 tablespoons. Add 1 lightly beaten egg, 1 cup raisins, and 1 tablespoon caraway seeds (optional) along with buttermilk. Bake to internal temperature of 170 degrees, 40 to 45 minutes, covering bread with aluminum foil if it is browning too much.

Figure 12.
Use a serrated knife to cut a cross shape in the top of the dough.
Each score should be 5 inches long and ¾ inch deep.

8 3

chapter nine

BANANA BREAD

OVERRIPE BANANAS ON THE KITCHEN counter are an excellent excuse to make banana bread. However, many banana breads are flat, gritty, or heavy. Even worse, some loaves taste only remotely of bananas. Good banana bread is soft and tender with plenty of banana flavor and crunchy toasted walnuts. It should be moist and light, something so delicious that you look forward to the bananas on the counter turning soft and mushy.

In our testing, we found it very important to pay close attention to the condition of the bananas. Sweet, older, darkly speckled bananas infused the bread with both moisture and flavor, which meant that the bread, whether still warm or day-old, succeeded with less butter than the amount used in most recipes.

We also experimented with the way we prepared the bananas for the batter: slightly mashed, mashed well, and pureed. Loaves with slightly mashed bananas left chunks of fruit. We preferred a smoother texture, but pureeing the bananas turned out to be a bad idea because the batter did not rise as well. Leavener probably escaped before the thin batter developed enough structure to trap gases. Bananas well-mashed by hand kept the batter thick.

We still wanted more moisture in the bread, so we tried mixing in milk, buttermilk, sour cream, and plain yogurt. Sour cream added richness, but it also made for a heavy texture and an unattractive, pebbly crust. Milk added little flavor and created a slick crust. Buttermilk added a delightful tang, but yogurt let the banana flavor stand out. And because yogurt has more solids than buttermilk, it made for a slightly more solid loaf, which we preferred.

While the added yogurt softened the bread's crumb, we still sought a more delicate, open texture. So we decided to experiment with various mixing methods to see how they affected the final texture. We considered the quick bread method and the creaming method (as defined on pages 17–18).

The creaming method created a soft texture (reminiscent of butter cake) and good volume from the whipped sugar and butter. However, its lighter color looked less appetizing next to the golden brown loaf achieved with the quick bread method. The quick bread method produced a delicate texture, too, and the less consistent crumb looked hearty and delicious. It also rose more than the creamed loaf. All in all, it was a better choice.

Take caution when mixing, though. When we stirred the wet and the dry ingredients into a smooth batter, the loaves turned out small and tough. Flour contains protein, and when protein mixes with water, gluten develops. The more you stir with a spoon, the more the gluten proteins arrange into long, orderly bundles. These bundles create an elastic batter that resists changing shape and cannot rise as well. To minimize gluten development, fold together the wet and dry ingredients gently, just until the dry ingredients are moistened. The batter should still be thick and chunky, but without any streaks of unincorporated flour.

Master Recipe

Banana Bread

makes one 9-inch loaf

➤ NOTE: *The success of this recipe depends on the use of very ripe bananas. Otherwise, the bread will be too dry. Toast the nuts on a baking sheet in a 350-degree oven until fragrant, about 6 minutes.*

	Vegetable cooking spray or unsalted butter for greasing loaf pan
2	cups all-purpose flour
¾	cup sugar
¾	teaspoon baking soda
½	teaspoon salt
3	very ripe, soft, darkly speckled large bananas, mashed well (about 1½ cups)
¼	cup plain yogurt
2	large eggs, beaten lightly
6	tablespoons unsalted butter, melted and cooled
1	teaspoon vanilla extract
1¼	cups toasted walnuts, chopped coarse (about 1 cup after chopping)

INSTRUCTIONS:

1. Adjust oven rack to lower-middle position and heat oven to 350 degrees. Grease and flour a 9 by 5-inch loaf pan; set aside.

2. Whisk flour, sugar, baking soda, and salt together in large bowl; set aside.

3. Mix mashed bananas, yogurt, eggs, butter, and vanilla with wooden spoon in medium bowl. Lightly fold banana mixture into dry ingredients with rubber spatula until just combined and batter looks thick and chunky. Fold in walnuts. Scrape batter into prepared loaf pan.

4. Bake until loaf is golden brown and toothpick inserted in center comes out clean, about 55 minutes. Cool in pan for 5 minutes, then transfer to wire rack. Serve warm or at room temperature. Once cooled, bread can be wrapped in plastic and stored at room temperature for a couple of days.

VARIATIONS:

Banana Chocolate Bread

Follow master recipe, reducing sugar to 10 tablespoons and adding 2½ ounces grated bittersweet chocolate (a heaping ½ cup) along with walnuts.

Banana Coconut Bread with Macadamia Nuts

Adjust oven rack to middle position and heat oven to 350 degrees. Toast ½ cup flaked, sweetened coconut and 1 cup chopped macadamia nuts on small cookie sheet, stirring every 2 minutes, until golden brown, about 6 minutes.

Follow master recipe, substituting toasted macadamias and coconut for walnuts.

Orange-Spice Banana Bread

Follow master recipe, adding 1 teaspoon ground cinnamon, ¼ teaspoon grated nutmeg, and 2 tablespoons grated orange zest to dry ingredients.

chapter ten

CRANBERRY NUT BREAD

WE DON'T MAKE CRANBERRY NUT BREAD just for ourselves. We make it for the kindergarten teacher, the mail carrier, and anyone else who deserves something homemade rather than store-bought for the holidays.

The problem is that this simple bread is often sub-par, sunken in the middle, too dense, or so overly sweetened that the contrast between the tart berries and what should be a slightly sweet dough is lost. We wanted to avoid these problems, and we had some other goals in mind as well. We were looking for a crust that was golden brown and evenly thin all the way around and a texture that was somewhere

90

between a dense, breakfast bread and a light, airy cake. And, for convenience sake, we wanted a recipe that fit easily into a standard 9 by 5-inch loaf pan. After looking at almost 60 recipes, it seemed evident that the mixing method and the leavening were the most important factors in getting the quick bread we were after.

First we tackled mixing. Some recipes called for the creaming method, others the quick bread method (as defined on pages 17–18). We made several loaves using each of these methods. While the creaming method did give us a marginally more tender bread, we quickly determined that it was too light and airy. We liked the denser, more compact texture produced by the quick bread method. An added advantage of the quick bread method is that—as its name implies—it can be put together very quickly.

Next we moved on to the question of leavening. When we looked back at our testing, we noted that 75 percent of the recipes combined baking powder with baking soda to leaven the bread. The rest used all baking powder or all baking soda. We tried every option we could think of using these two leaveners, both alone and together. We found that baking powder seemed to enhance the flavor, while baking soda supported the structure; finding the right balance was tricky. Eventually, we came to the decision that ¼ teaspoon of baking soda combined with 1 teaspoon of baking powder gave us the bright flavor and rather dense texture we were looking for.

With our mixing and leavening methods settled, we focused on ingredients. We quickly determined that we liked the flavor that butter provided over that of oil, margarine, or vegetable shortening. More than one egg made the bread almost too rich and caused the interior to turn somewhat yellow. After testing different amounts and types of sugar, we stuck with one cup of granulated sugar, which provided the right amount of sweetness. Orange zest added not only to the flavor but to the interior appearance as well.

We also tinkered with the liquid component. Many recipes called for water or even boiling water, but freshly squeezed orange juice was usually mentioned and offered the best flavor. We compared fresh, home-squeezed orange juice with commercially prepared juices made from both fresh oranges and from concentrate; home-squeezed juice was the winner, hands down.

Not every recipe called for dairy, but we tested everything from heavy cream to sour cream. Both buttermilk and yogurt provided the moistness and tang we were looking for, with buttermilk edging out yogurt by a hairbreadth.

Last but not least were the cranberries. The cranberry harvest begins just after Labor Day and continues through early fall, which means that by mid- to late January, no fresh berries are available. Cranberries freeze beautifully, so grab a few extra bags to have on hand and freeze them until ready to use. We found no discernible difference in the finished product whether using fresh or frozen cranberries.

Cranberry Nut Bread

makes one 9-inch loaf

➤ **NOTE:** *We prefer sweet, mild pecans in this bread, but walnuts can be substituted. Resist the urge to cut into the bread while it is hot out of the oven; the texture improves as it cools, making it easier to slice. To toast pecans, place skillet over medium heat, add chopped pecans, and toast, shaking pan frequently, until nuts are fragrant, 3 to 5 minutes.*

	Vegetable cooking spray or unsalted butter for greasing loaf pan
1	tablespoon grated orange zest
⅓	cup fresh orange juice
⅔	cup buttermilk
6	tablespoons unsalted butter, melted and cooled
1	large egg, beaten lightly
2	cups all-purpose flour
1	cup sugar
1	teaspoon salt
1	teaspoon baking powder
¼	teaspoon baking soda
1½	cups cranberries (about 6 ounces), chopped coarse
½	cup pecans, chopped coarse and toasted

INSTRUCTIONS:

1. Adjust oven rack to middle position and heat oven to 375 degrees. Grease and flour a 9 by 5-inch loaf pan; set aside.

2. Stir together orange zest, orange juice, buttermilk, butter, and egg in small bowl. Whisk together flour, sugar, salt, baking powder, and baking soda in large bowl. Stir liquid ingredients into dry with rubber spatula until just moistened. Gently stir in cranberries and pecans. Do not overmix. Scrape batter into loaf pan and spread with rubber spatula into corners of pan.

3. Bake 20 minutes, then reduce heat to 350 degrees; continue to bake until golden brown and toothpick inserted in center of loaf comes out clean, about 45 minutes longer. Cool in pan 10 minutes, then transfer to wire rack and cool at least 1 hour before serving. Once cooled, bread can be wrapped in plastic and stored at room temperature for a couple of days.

index